AF342339

Peace & Blessings

Michael A. Price, Jr.
2/9/2009 A.D.

# Right In Front Of You

# Right In Front Of You:
# Uncommon Sense in Poetry

## Michael A. Price, Jr.

Uncommon Sense Publishing

Copyright © 2008 by Michael A. Price, Jr.

Cover design by Marrimarra
Book design by Marrimarra

Book layout by All American Printing Inc., Alexandria, VA



Printed in the United States of America

First Printing: November 2008

ISBN-978-0-9791406-2-4

Uncommon Sense Publishing Company

This book is dedicated to the life and legacy of
Mr. Harry Lee Jackson, Jr.


*"You've got to make your spirit overtake your flesh."*
-Harry Lee Jackson, Jr.

# Introduction

Common sense is dead. It just does not exist in the world we live anymore. There was a time when the people who had sense were the majority. But as time passes, those who either don't think or don't care seem to be outnumbering the rest of us. Because those who have sense are now in the minority, it can no longer be called 'common sense'. What seems to be a more accurate term for having a measure of wisdom is 'uncommon sense'.

This book aims to shed some light on issues that happen *right in front of you* and tries to provide thought provoking insight in a poetic format. The writings are divided into three sections. The first section covers various subjects that people deal with in everyday life situations. The second section confronts contemporary issues and politics in America. The final section provides an insight on matters of a spiritual nature.

Each poem is preceded by a brief introduction; which helps to give some background to its theme, as well as what inspired me to write it.

For those who are searching for answers, I hope that these writings are able to help you guide yourself to where you want to be.

For those who already have wisdom, please join me in an effort to overpower the ignorance, malice, and stupidity in this world; so that we can make 'uncommon sense', common again.

# Table of Contents

# LIFE

# Your Word is Your Bond

Many people say they'll do things that they don't actually do. This poem addresses the importance of the relationship between word and deed.

# Your Word is Your Bond

You don't need to give your word,
If indeed you *live* your word.
Do what you say you'll do,
You'll be respected when you're heard.

You shouldn't have to 'swear to God',
For you to gain an accepting nod.
To be compelled to do that,
Shows that there is something odd.

If your character is honest,
It's unnecessary to promise.
Living by a moral standard,
Isn't only for the Amish.

When you're walking in the truth,
It becomes a living proof.
Your integrity protects you,
Like the shelter of a roof.

If you say your word is your bond,
Watch the words you're standing on.
Since they serve as your foundation,
Keep it true to make it strong.

When your word and deeds relate,
You can win any debate.
For a person who walks the talk,
Is someone **no one** can negate.

In a world of false projections,
That are driven by deceptions,
It is very difficult,
To gain an accurate perception.

Once you find the right way through it,
Give an effort to not add to it.
Keep you words in sync with life,
As best as you are able to do it.

# The Power of Silence

Everybody knows somebody that just does not know when to shut up. The inspiration for this one came from people I know that just talk without listening, instead of actually having a conversation.

# The Power of Silence

It's often more prudent for you to say less,
Over saying much too much.
Sometimes the solution that is best,
Is knowing when just to hush!

Many people in time have met their demise,
With the hot air from out of their lungs.
Though even a fool is thought to be wise,
When he learns to hold his tongue.

How many times have we heard it said?
Yet to many, it hasn't occurred,
To save all that talking coming out of your head,
'Cause *actions speak louder than words.*

If it cannot display, in a non-verbal way,
Then it's childish, and mentally weak.
You still can convey, what you have to say,
Without always having to speak.

Sometimes a glance can state your case,
Or simply just using your hands.
Even the way that you shape your face,
Without words, they'll still understand.

If you just talk, then you just wouldn't know,
There are so many things that you're missin'.
See you cannot grow, with your mouth on the go,
'Cause you only can learn when you listen!

Sometimes it *is* best to say it with sound,
Sometimes it's to just keep it shut.
The essence of wisdom can truly be found,
In knowing when to do what.

So the next time you have a point to make,
Please give this a shot, and try it;
To avoid the aches of such verbal mistakes,
Try to say it, while still being quiet.

# Watch Your Kids

This poem discusses the virtues of instilling discipline in your young ones, and the consequences for failing to do so.

# Watch Your Kids

You need to watch your kids,
Because they're watching you;
Hearing all that you say,
Learning from what you do.
When they're acting too wild,
You better handle that child!
If you stand in denial,
They'll be standing on trial.


You need to watch you kids.
You don't do them a favor,
When you do not forbid,
Them from foolish behavior;
Acting out in the store,
Throwing tantrums on floors,
Even when they ignore,
What you're calling them for.

You need to watch your kids,
Instead of watching TV,
Or the wrong that they did,
Could turn to what they will be.
'Cause in less than a minute,
They will test all your limits,
And they'll push further in it,
Just to see if you meant it.


You need to watch your kids.
Make sure they understand,
That they've got to comply,
With the laws of the land.
Or they'll be going to school,
Acting like a damn fool,
Breaking all of the rules,
And really thinking it's cool.

You need to watch your kids,
And what they get into.
Although they need your love,
They need discipline too.
Playing like they don't hear?
Put their hind parts in gear!
Gotta use pain or fear,
To make sure they adhere.


You need to watch your kids,
'Cause there's nothing that's worse,
Than a spoiled little brat,
Making you hear *him* first!
Whether son or a daughter,
Must establish some order.
Making sure they have borders,
Helps them do what they oughtta.

You need to watch your kids.
Please don't make others do it.
You let them do what they want,
As a parent, you blew it.
'Cause they'll live all their life,
Thinking that it's alright,
To do whatever they like,
As if they have the right.


You need to watch your kids,
'Cause when they become older,
Things that you should have done,
Will weigh hard on your shoulders.
It's while they're young to instill,
A sense of their social skills.
If you don't teach them to chill,
Then the law surely will.

# Anger Management

This one really doesn't need much of an introduction. The title says it all.

# Anger Management

Have you ever been so mad at someone,
And the rage took over your head;
That if at the time, your hand had a gun,
The person would probably be dead?

If you know what it feels like to be there,
Then it's easy for you to understand,
Why it's so important for us to beware,
When your anger can get out of hand.

There are people whose lives are a mess,
And are mentally and spiritually off center.
So when having to deal with a conflict or stress,
They resort to respond with their temper.

Anger surely impacts on your mind,
With a grip that's like money or sex.
Its seductive power can make people blind,
To its often destructive effects.

Like the force of a demonic spirit,
It hungers for your life and your soul.
If you make the mistake of listening when you hear it,
You'll be tempted to give it control.

It feels great when you let the rage flow,
And the wrath has a hold of your senses.
But when you come back after having let go,
What you did could have harsh consequences.

I'm not saying that you shouldn't get upset,
'Cause that would be unrealistic.
Just think not to do anything you'll regret,
Before you start going ballistic.

If you don't think it puts you in danger,
Here's a question to give you a clue:
Do you have a problem with managing anger,
Or do problems with anger *have you?*

# The Fix

I have probably drank and smoked too much in my lifetime to come across as righteously indignant to those who still do. However, this one is dedicated to people who do it to avoid dealing with some major problem that really needs their sober attention.

# The Fix

Sometimes when you're walking through the valleys of life,
It can be hell to handle the hardships and strife.
But the worst thing to do when you're dealing with stress,
Is to alter the state of your consciousness.

Seductive, destructive, sick, sad, and pathetic,
If you attempt to escape by using street anesthetics.
It's a temporary fix, but it won't break your fall,
When you try to heal hurts with drugs and alcohol.

You can drink till the pain in your senses diminish,
The issues will still be right there when you finish.
You could snort all the coke till your nose leaves your face,
Your problems in life will remember their place.

Taking ecstasy pills make you feel like you're healed,
But you'll really fell ill when you deal in the real.
Even if you smoked weed till you're high as the clouds,
The voice of your troubles will speak just as loud.

Any method that's used as a means of escape,
Is an illusion that most addicts seem to create.
You can run as far away as you are able to get to,
The things you run from *will still be right there with you*!

Anyone who's been there knows I'm speaking the truth.
I don't care if the liquor is one eighty proof;
Or the shipment you got is the best of its kind,
It's a dangerous game to play tricks on your mind.

The way out of the struggles, the pain, and the trials,
Can't be found in a bottle, a baggie, or vial;
But in looking at your troubles with a clear sober head,
For a better way to cope, and to move you ahead.

It's of utmost importance to get help about it,
If you feel you're unable to function without it.
Best to face all the unresolved problems you're battling,
'Cause there's no real escape from yourself, or reality.

# To Love Someone

What book of poems would be complete
without one on Love?

# To Love Someone

Written about in magazines.
Fictionalized on TV screens.
But in dealing with facts,
There are many who lack,
Understanding of what love means.


Whether coming from your mother,
Family, friend, a spouse, or lover;
It's the word we say,
As a means to convey,
Strong feelings for one another.


But what a person may profess,
Compares to what they manifest,
Can contradict,
And make one sick,
From the heartaches, hurt, and stress.

Love, has much to do with giving,
And learning how to be forgiving.
It's being there for,
Those you care for.
It's what makes this life worth living.


Standing strong when a problem rises.
Helping out throughout the crisis.
Taking the trouble,
To aid their struggle,
And making sacrifices.


Love will lead you to defend,
When you're needed as a friend;
To help them cope.
To give them hope,
And support through thick and thin.

Love is often glamorized.
Many fail to realize,
That it only works,
When the other comes first,
And looking at life through their eyes.


It's an investment of yourself,
For the sake of someone else.
It's an earnest desire,
To lift someone higher,
To improve their life and health.


It doesn't seem to make much sense,
To do it at your own expense.
Such an expression,
Would surely lessen,
The walls of your self-defense.

But we're not meant to be alone,
Or have a heart that's made of stone.
We're here to share,
Our life affairs;
Not out there on our own.


It's easy to love when things are well.
That's why it's really hard to tell,
If what you feel,
Is truly real,
Until you've gone through hell.


But even when it isn't fun,
It's holding on till the storm is done.
Those are the stakes,
Of what it takes,
When you really love someone.

# Sex Sells

One morning, I woke up early and turned on the television. There was a televangelist on, so I figured I may get a message to start the day. After a few minutes, the program goes to a commercial break. The very first commercial is a saucy ad for Victoria's Secret's new line of lingerie. After seeing the 'gears chance so fast', I thought to myself, 'Damn, sex sells.'

# Sex Sells

Big beautiful breasts and bodacious butts.
Lean long luscious legs and lascivious lusts.

Voluptuous videos unveil volumes of vanity,
With gyrating jiggles jilting guys to insanity.

Advertisements add ass as allure and attraction.
Selling sexual sights, serving pseudo-satisfaction.

Obviously objectified over obsessions of others,
Reality reveals sisters, daughters, and mothers.

While we wondrously watch women with wanton wishes,
Fools fall for fantasies forgetting that it's fictitious.

Big businesses believe bucks are brought by the babes.
Provocative poses persuade people to pay;

For the power to possess products that bring promiscuous pleasures,
Many men are manipulated for their monetary measures.

So when you sense some sales pitch seducing you, stop it.
Keep sex in its context, and out of your pocket.

# The Words We Use

This poem discusses some commonly used curse words and the perils in using them. Although this is the last poem in this book that has profanity, I felt it necessary to use the bad words for the sake of expressing how dangerous they can be. The point being that they are called curse words for a reason!

# The Words We Use

There's life, and death, in the words that we use.
While some can build, others surely abuse.
We must be more mindful, and not get confused;
'Cause there's too much at stake, and too much to lose.

It's so easy to use words, and though that's a fact,
Once they leave from your mouth, you can't take them back.
And each slur you put out there, since they don't retract,
Can bite back at you hard once your Karma attacks.

Remember that time that you called her a 'bitch'?
You put scars on her spirit that just couldn't be stitched.
If your mother, or your daughter, was referred to like this,
You would look for who said it, 'cause you'd really be pissed!

And when you hear 'fuck you!', there's nowhere to go;
Except to a weapon, or coming to blows!
The sting never leaves; it just festers and grows,
Whether coming from a stranger, or someone you know.

And that word called 'nigger' is probably the worst,
'Cause of where it came from, and who used it first.
It mocks the ancestors and all of their hurts,
By continuing to fuel the generational curse.

You can strip one's esteem with the words that are said;
You could push one to angers that make them see red;
You can rip someone's guts out, and make them feel dead;
Without even touching a hair on their head.

To do so is cruel; the outcome demonic.
Since almost all do it, the problem is chronic.
These words that spew out of the mouth, like hot vomit,
Contaminate our world, and all that are on it.

We must be more mindful, and not get confused;
'Cause there's too much at stake, and too much to lose.
It's best to use caution with the phrasings you choose,
'Cause there's life, and death, in the words that we use.

# The Pursuit of Happiness

Isn't the desire for happiness the main
reason for almost everything that we do?
If it isn't, then shouldn't it be?

# The Pursuit of Happiness

We all just want to have a good time.
There's nothing wrong with that.
So do what you must so you can find,
Where your happiness is at.

The feeling that puts you at your best,
That makes you jump and scream!
Do not let yourself settle for less.
Keep trying to reach your dreams.

Remember the last time you had,
That truly made you smile?
There's many people mad,
Because it's been too long a while.

Some folks are wound up way too tight,
And seem intensely furious;
Not realizing that they might,
Just take themselves too serious.

In carrying around all of that stress,
They probably need a breather.
But the acquisition of happiness,
Is the ultimate reliever.

The greatest gift that you can have,
Is not a material toy;
But really knowing how to laugh,
And how to feel real joy.

I ask this question for your sake,
So you don't stay feeling numb:
What is it that it's gonna take,
For you to have some fun?!?

So whatever you need to enjoy yourself,
By all means, go pursue it.
As long as you, or no one else,
Gets damaged while you do it.

# Generational Relations

The purpose of this poem is to remind
people that we are standing on the
shoulders of our ancestors.

# Generational Relations

The newest branch on the tree;
The latest link in the chain;
Is what you happen to be.
Continue keeping the flame.

Your ancestors had to strive.
Some had to suffer in pain.
Some even gave up their lives,
To have the things you attained.

If they could talk to you now,
Then they would surely explain;
And let you know of just how,
To keep the struggle sustained.

Though they may be dead and gone,
It's through you that they remain.
Their legacy still lives on,
Since their blood runs through your veins.

You're not just here for yourself,
Or just to be entertained,
Nor for your personal wealth;
This life is more than a game.

You're an extension of them,
In spirit, one and the same.
You can uplift or condemn,
The family from which you came.

They *need* you to understand,
This message simple and plain:
Their hopes are now in your hands,
And how you carry their name.

So don't forget what they've done,
'Cause that would bring them to shame.
Remember where you come from.
Don't let their works be in vain.

# Continuum

This poem describes how the
choices of today turn into the
outcomes of tomorrow.

# Continuum

Yesterday was once today.
Today will flow into tomorrow.
The ability to see that they're interconnected,
Will determine your joy or sorrow.

Seconds swiftly turn into a minute.
Sixty minutes is the size of an hour.
Planning of how it should best be used,
Is the way to harness its power.

Time, is much like a river that flows;
Only going in a single direction.
There's nothing anybody can do that would change,
The course of its forward projection.

But as far as the path of our lives are concerned,
We are able to have more control.
As the 'master of your fate', it's on you to get to,
The place of your dreams and your goals.

Whether you're aware that it's happening or not,
You make choices throughout the day.
And each of these choices can steer your life,
In a positive or negative way.

Yet there is one choice that is guaranteed,
To put your life in a stall;
And that's by making the worst mistake,
Of doing nothing at all.

Since your future depends on your action right now,
It's best that you do **you** a favor;
By making the choice of committing yourself,
To change self-destructive behavior.

Time is the stuff that your life is made of.
Decisions affect how it's spent.
Understanding their impact will help you fulfill,
The purpose for what it was meant.

# AMERICA

# Desensitization

This poem was inspired by the redundancy of the negative events covered in the news, and our increasingly detached reactions to it.

# Desensitization

Each time I sit and watch the news,
It seems the reporters would say,
A different, but same type tragedy,
They spoke of yesterday.

A President has started war,
On someone else's soil.
American blood values more than Iraqi,
But not as much as oil.

The district has built a new stadium;
Education, a lesser place.
Backward priorities reveals,
Our 'Nationals' disgrace.

A congressional bureaucracy,
That always moves in slow motion;
Yet every time they get a chance,
They give themselves pay promotions.

An inflated housing market,
In the capital of the nation.
Less chocolate in chocolate city,
Due to modern gentrification.

Thousands lost homes from hurricanes.
In front of our TV, we shed tears.
A homeless man asks for money at the metro,
But that, we pretend not to hear.

It seems the farther away the problem,
The more we are sympathetic.
Yet when up close, Apathy
Has now become America's new epidemic.

The question is no longer what went wrong,
Or even if things are fair.
The biggest problem in our world today,
Is if we the people, care.

# The Problems with Politics

There was yet another political scandal that was coming out when this one was written.

# The Problems with Politics

If fidelity and fairness frame our freedom's foundation,
Why are wrongdoings rampant with our representation?

Politicians present pledges and promises to people.
Expressed eloquence in elections to treat us even and equal.

Lots of leaders and lawmakers lack long lasting luster.
Ineffective forces fight flustered for their failed filibusters.

Congressional corruption causes contempt and criticism.
Negatives of nationalism nudge us next to nihilism.

Government greatness gets grounded by the grip of greed's gravity.
Manipulating morality to manage men as their majesty.

Double-standards by dollars demonizes democracy.
Having hellish hubris to hold hands with hypocrisy.

The citizens are sick of seeing strings of such scandals.
Hearing how often it happens is too heavy to handle.

The future is fading fast for our federal faith.
Leaders must live moral laws, before it's too late.

# Monetary Mayhem

Inspired by the state of the
American economy in 2008.

# Monetary Mayhem

You don't have to be a financial professor,
To notice the dollar is buying you lesser.
It seems we're all facing additional pressure,
To handle the rising costs.

Our wallets are hemorrhaging under the stress,
In figuring out how to deal with this mess.
The things we've spent most our lives to invest,
Could all be potentially lost.

From the gas to the groceries, the prices skyrocket.
The experts have yet to figure how to stop it.
These issues keep digging deeper in our pocket,
And taking what little is in it.

Bills that cannot be covered by personal pension,
Are causing us all to experience tension.
Can barely afford to even pay attention,
Our budgets are stretched to the limit.

It isn't the people who make the decisions,
Or those we get news from on the television,
That are getting the worst of inflation's condition.
The impact is not as severe;

As the ones who are living paycheck to paycheck,
With poverty breathing down the back of their neck,
That are catching the brunt of the rippling effects,
And struggling to get in the clear.

Our economy's future at this point looks bleak.
The strength of our money is increasingly weak.
Each household is working its hardest to seek,
A way to cope in this recession.

But until the dollar can regain its might,
We'll fasten our belt buckles slightly more tight,
And hope that the system can set itself right,
Before we go into depression.

# Ode to Obama

This poem addresses the unprecedented
political phenomenon known as
Barack Hussein Obama II.
(*written prior to his election*)

# Ode to Obama

Whoever would have thought,
That Obama would make,
A run to be the President of the United States?

He has a helluva shot.
It seems to be in his range.
He's the epitome of everything to do with change.

Which causes some concerns.
We want to understand,
All the issues that are out there and of where he'll stand.

But he knows how to relate.
He has developed the sense.
His lineage is like a link of all the continents.

He's related to me.
He's related to you.
He's related to a Buddhist monk in Katmandu.

All the relations he has,
Gives him political glow.
He's like a walking social spectrum of the whole rainbow.

And that could help us all out,
'Cause it can be a good thing.
Bridging gaps is something that he can potentially bring.

And with a story like his,
Maybe he'll stand for us all.
Especially if he is careful not to drop the ball.

Some people think he'll mess up.
I'm really wondering how.
He couldn't possibly screw up more than the one there now.

Though politics are corrupt,
Let's hope he's worthy of trust,
And that his leadership could help connect the rest of us.

# American Soldier

Solemnly dedicated to all of
our soldiers involved in the
Iraq invasion.

# American Soldier

American soldier
Young and green
Caught up in the war machine

Apple pie
Fourth of July
Some will kill and others die

Nine-eleven
Terrorism
Fear turned into patriotism

Pledge of allegiance
Send a legion
To a far and foreign region

American soldier
At attention
Military intervention

Shock and awe
A mighty force
Rider of the pale white horse

Fight for the nation
Strange location
Rape, blood, death, and mutilation

Half the monster
Half the victim
Propaganda surely tricked 'em

American soldier
On a mission
Sent there by our politicians

Afghanistan
I understand
Bin Ladin and the Taliban

But not in Iraq
We're wrong on that
Too late for us to take it back

Commander in chief
Has caused us grief
Can't win a war against beliefs

American soldier
The injured bleeds
Impact from the IEDs

Islamic God
Will send a squad
Suicide attack for their Jihad

Too numb to feel
Some parts are still
Left out on that battlefield

The death toll rises
High gas prices
Worth our human sacrifices

American soldier
Growing older
Heavy conscience on their shoulders

Government backing
For attacking
Countless dead among Iraqis

Away and alone
Far from home
Lifeline through the telephone

The tours are too long
For staying strong
Within a land they don't belong

American soldier
Families nervous
Praying they'll return from service

To risk their neck
They've earned respect
Need our help to reconnect

American soldier
Fought and served
Our country owes what they deserve

By making sure
We don't fight for
Unnecessary wars no more.

# The Tempest
## (Anger of the Oppressed)

There are many angry have-nots in the world. This poem draws comparisons between their surging rage and an imminent natural disaster.

# The Tempest
## (Anger of the Oppressed)

Thunder cracking in their ears.
Pressure mounting over years.
Motivated by their fears.
Damage done has been severe.

Darkened clouds engulf the skies.
Morals become compromised.
Many multi-layered lies.
Nature's temper on the rise.

A volcano will explode.
Senses stuck on overload.
Led them down a long wrong road.
Only pride left to uphold.

Lava coursing through their veins.
Migraine headache hurricanes.
Circumstance against the grain.
Mental muscles full of pain.

Trapped beneath the false ideals.
Others don't know how it feels,
When your soul is blizzard chill,
And what's wrong becomes what's real.

An emotional monsoon,
Will begin to fill this room,
And all here will be consumed,
If we don't address them soon.

A tornado passing through.
All contrition overdue.
And most haven't got a clue.
Wonder what they're gonna do?

'Cause a storm is on its way,
And it won't be kept at bay.
If we don't hear what they say,
It will blow this world away.

# Police and the People

An honest assessment of the state
of affairs between police officers
and the citizens they protect.

# Police and the People

Our officers patrol the land,
To keep us safe as best they can;
However they must understand,
The power that they wield.

In having that authority,
They must have sensitivity,
Of the responsibility,
That comes with gun and shield.

Police that do respect their role,
May they be blessed a hundred fold,
For what they do to help uphold,
The laws of where we are.

But there's a few that will abuse,
And find a way to break the rules,
By acting however they choose,
And pushing things too far.

Some fail to use some common sense,
And make the situation tense,
By causing uncalled for offense.
Their reputation precedes them.

But where the *real* criminals go,
It can take long for them to show.
Their response time can be too slow,
In being there when we need them.

Although we should all have respect,
For those who do serve and protect,
The way they do their job affects,
The way we feel about them.

May there be improved relations,
Between them and the population,
'Cause order in our civilization,
Probably wouldn't exist, without them.

# The "Dubya" Limericks

A limerick is a certain style of poem. One of the most popular ones starts as "There once was a man from Nantucket". Limericks are usually humorous and satirical. This one is a summary of the eight years under the Presidency of George Walker Bush.

# The "Dubya" Limericks

There once was a leader named George,
Who dug holes for us deep as a gorge.
As he wraps up his terms,
Let us see what we've learned,
From the legacy that he has forged.

He had shade with him from the beginning,
And the controversy of his winning.
'Cause the Florida governor,
Happened to be his brother,
There's suspicion of dark underpinnings.

Since the day of his inauguration,
He's put us in some bad situations.
His political blunders,
Have taken us under,
With the weight of his administration.

It's been said that he snorted cocaine;
Which just seems like it's totally insane,
That so many voted,
For a guy who got loaded,
And the highest office he obtained.

There are problems that George failed to answer.
Take for instance Katrina's disaster.
With the lack of respect,
And the criminal neglect,
New Orleans should have heard from him much faster.

George had pressed that Iraq be invaded,
Despite what many others debated;
But the weapons weren't there,
Now it's like a nightmare,
That he surely underestimated.

He made tax breaks for wealthy and rich,
So that they could get more with no hitch.
But the less that you earn,
As far as he's concerned,
You might as well go and jump in a ditch.

Like a king who sat high in a tower,
George corruptly abused all his power.
When the law said he couldn't,
He did things that he shouldn't;
Which is why his relations are sour.

George has pushed agendas of his mission,
With a very narrow field of vision.
If you don't go along,
Then you're labeled as wrong,
And an enemy of true patriotism.

George has left many people annoyed;
Handling problems like he's a cowboy.
And has so often lacked,
To use much needed tact,
His departure will bring many joy.

He has come across as a deceiver.
Tricky tactics fooled many believers.
People from other lands,
Have a similar stance.
They don't seem to like him that much either.

Many people think that George is dumb.
It looks more that he seems to be numb;
Like he just doesn't care,
For those that do not share,
The same background of where he came from.

George has overlooked so many people.
He did not reflect everyone equal.
But in '04 he wins,
The high office again,
Like a bad movie having a sequel.

Now his rate of approval is sinking.
People finally notice something stinking.
When you gave him your vote,
You helped him sink our boat.
What the hell were you people all thinking?!?

Though we're glad that his tenure is ending,
The impact that he left is still pending.
He caused many ordeals.
Only time will reveal,
All the problems we'll need to be mending.

His poor judgment will sorely affect us.
Let's just hope that the good Lord protects us;
And that it's not too late,
To get our country straight,
When he packs up and heads back to Texas.

# Cracks in the American Dream

An acknowledgement of the people who
live in the shadow of the American ideals.

# Cracks in the American Dream

In our quest to achieve the American dream,
There's millions who have fallen through the cracks and seams.
Most of their stories are seldom ever mentioned,
Yet their lives are still in need of some attention.

There are people who are hopelessly addicted to drugs,
That cannot seem to climb out of the hole they've dug.
Or the ones that feel they've had to deal with so much strife,
That they've given up, and thinking how to end their life.

And what about the children with no one to guide them,
That desperately need someone to be there beside them?
Or the ones who spend their golden years in nursing homes,
Who are hardly ever visited, or telephoned?

Some people live in poverty that grips so hard,
That they can't see any farther than from where they are.
Or the ones that need a doctor, but may be so poor,
That they can't get any treatment 'cause they're uninsured.

We can't overlook the people with no place to live,
That survive off what we throw away, or what we give.
Or the families affected by the hurricanes,
There's no words that can describe all of their loss and pain.

Let's not forget the people locked inside the penn.
They're human, despite what they did that got them in.
Or the women of the night that have themselves for sale,
Which puts them and their families through a living hell.

All of the people mentioned have something they share;
Unless they are related to you, most don't care.
Their lives have as much value as both yours and mine.
Them being disregarded is a moral crime.

When you hear yourself complain of how your life ain't fair,
There's people who have less that should be in your prayers.
Respect the pain and suffering that some go through,
'Cause there's no guarantee tomorrow, that it won't be you.

# Doing Something about It

Dedicated to all of the social and
political prognosticators.

# Doing Something about It

Everybody has some words about the problems;
Going on and on and on of how to solve them.
But speaking in itself is no solution,
Unless it leads to positive conclusions.

If you are great at word articulation,
Your audience may show appreciation.
But even if the venue is really crowded,
It still boils down to what you'll do about it.

Though it *sounds* good in human interaction,
Those words must all be followed up with action!
As verbal leaders come a dime a dozen,
Effective, is a trait they often wasn't.

In talking yourself up to being a hero,
The impact may equate to almost zero.
Most people are inclined and tend to doubt it;
Unless you really do something about it.

For a message to be seen as being consistent,
Advice should also come with your assistance.
'Cause that provides the people with some proof,
To know the words you're speaking as the truth.

Just merely talking about a bad situation,
Is futile to the point of irritation.
It's by your deeds that your word's worth is counted;
Which is why you must do something about it.

We have so many issues to be tending.
The list of them is almost never ending.
So if you think you truly have the answer,
To one of the many social plagues and cancers,

Then roll your sleeves and work to make it happen!
To demonstrate that you can be the captain.
'Cause only then will skeptics not be clouded,
In witnessing you've done something about it.

# The Sonnet of Our Nation

*Our Country is far from perfect,
but it's still Our Country!*

# The Sonnet of Our Nation

Our Country is the only home we have.
There is no other place I'd rather be;
But yet it seems we're headed down a path,
That threatens everything that makes us free.
Our nation is an ideal to uphold,
That must live first within our hearts and minds.
But right and wrong can now be bought and sold,
Which causes patriotism to decline.
Our civic duties ought to be made clear,
In terms that 'we the people' understand.
Aside from you just merely being here,
What good do you contribute to this land?
America can only be as strong,
As loyal citizens to whom belongs.

# SPIRITUALITY

# Be Grateful

Simply for the sake of appreciation.

# Be Grateful

Each time that you wake,
Each breath that you take,
Each step that you make,
　　Be Grateful.

Each year that you grow,
Each fact that you know,
Each place that you go,
　　Be Grateful.

Each meal that you eat,
Each friend that you meet,
Each of your heartbeats,
　　Be Grateful.

Each day, you're alive!
Each day, you survive!
Each day that you thrive,
　　Be Grateful!

Each time you were burned,
From making wrong turns;
You've lived and you've learned.
　　Be Grateful.

Each tear that you've shed,
From when you were misled,
You're still moving ahead.
Be Grateful.

Though this world isn't fair,
And it's full of despair;
Your life has been spared.
Be Grateful.

The good Lord is with you.
It's by Him that you get through.
So in all you get into,
Be Grateful.

# Vindication of the Righteous

'Nice guys finish last.' 'Only the good die young.' Age old sayings such as these have led people to think that it's stupid to do what you feel is right. This one is meant to encourage those who are keeping the light of righteousness in the midst of the darkness of this world.

# Vindication of the Righteous

It seems somewhere down the line,
Like doing right,
Lost its might;
While those that plot to do wrong,
Are more respected as strong.

The ways of this wicked world,
Seem to reward,
Those who horde;
But those who are positive,
Must struggle harder to live.

It really is all screwed up.
We treat the meek,
Like they're weak;
And those who often raise hell,
Get treated better and well.

No wonder we're such a mess.
We idolize,
Our demise;
By treating righteousness worse,
And putting jackasses first.

These people sneer at your merit,
And use your virtue,
To hurt you;
To make you think crooked deeds,
Is the best way to succeed.

It's easier to do wrong,
When you don't care,
What is fair;
And trying to make others do,
Things to accommodate you.

But when you want to do right,
It isn't easy.
Believe me.
At times you'll be there alone,
And often left on your own.

But don't be fooled by it all.
They'll surely pay,
For their ways.
Darkness always tries to force,
Good people off of their course.

Please don't abandon your morals.
It's what God gave you,
To save you;
To make you be more aware,
Of all the evil out there.

And at the end of it all,
You'll be the winner,
To sinners;
And known as one of the greatest.
Triumphantly vindicated.

# Deliverance

The inspiration for this poem came from having to find my way past a devastating and life changing incident.

# Deliverance

Whatever it is that had caught you off guard,
Or that made you fall hard,
Or that left your heart scarred;

Whenever it was that your joy disappeared,
And that filled you with tears,
Be it weeks, months, or years;

Wherever it is that you misplaced your hope,
At the end of your rope,
As you struggle to cope;

Whoever it is that is duly to blame,
As the cause of your pain,
For their personal gain;

However you got to that dark dismal place,
That put lines on your face,
Or that caused you disgrace;

You must realize that you're caught in a snare,
And if you're not aware,
It will keep you right there.

You may still be stuck in that moment in time,
At the scene of the crime,
In your heart and your mind.

Those thoughts of regret will turn into a prison,
If you make the decision,
To stay in that condition.

We've all been through things that have hurt in the past,
But the question to ask,
'How long you'll let it last?!'

The life that you live is just time that is borrowed.
While you drown in your sorrow,
It will jinx your tomorrow!

Those demons will feed off the wounds once inflicted.
They will act unrestricted,
Till you have them evicted.

Do **not** let despair make you hide under covers.
You must fight to recover!
In some way or another.

For the love of your life, find the keys to your cell,
And break out of that jail!
And climb up from that hell!

And once you've broke free from the trap you were in,
You'll find strength from within,
To start living again.

# You Are Not Just Blessed for You

Although I consider myself to be a God fearing person, I have found myself getting annoyed at affluent Christians seeming to brag on what they've got. This one is for them.

# You Are Not Just Blessed for You

To all of God's children whom much has been given,
Take a moment to think of the way that you're livin'.
Are you praising the Lord with your singing and dances?
But not with *real* help, nor with your finances?

It's easy to thank Him when you're sitting pretty,
But what of the others in need in your city?
The message I'm trying to help you get to,
Is that you are not just blessed for you.

There are many people whose lives have been broken,
Yet their plight usually goes unspoken.
Since they often don't have the almighty dollar,
Then no one else hears their screams or their hollers.

If you say you are blessed, and highly favored,
Then it ought to reflect in your helpful behavior!
Other people should benefit from the good works you do,
'Cause you are not just blessed for you.

Your favored claim is no privilege, or right,
But a responsibility to carry the light.
And some well-to-do Christians may seem to get nervous,
If they mute the Lord's voice when He calls them to service.

For those who are lost, and in need of direction,
Your active assistance should bring forth a reflection;
Of the right way to go, and to help them get through,
'Cause you are not just blessed for you.

A great deal of folks are caught in a crisis,
And need living examples to see who Christ is.
If we give them His words without living the letters,
Then we really can't act like we're that much better.

In fact, it's *worse* to sit idle on blessings,
And ignore the problems that we should be addressing.
Though the Lord calls us all, the chosen are few,
'Cause you are not just blessed, for you.

# Double Edged Words

An analysis of the strange double
meanings of some commonly used
words in the English language.

# Double Edged Words

Have you ever noticed certain words,
Found in the dictionary,
Have peculiar types,
Of double meanings that they carry?

Even when their spellings differ,
They can sound the same.
The different meanings they have,
Seem to play tricks on the brain.

The definition of the 'sole',
Refers to underneath,
The lowest part of you found at,
The bottom of your feet.

And there is your eternal 'Soul',
The other term we know.
Below you is the last place that,
You would want it to go.

A 'prophet' speaks the word of God,
Yet 'profit' means make money.
Confusing cash for wisdom,
Seems to strike as oddly funny.

To be 'whole' means to be complete;
And 'hole' means missing something.
So if you're holy, does it mean,
You're godly, or you're wanting?

'Peace' is calm tranquility,
And 'piece' is just a fraction.
But every 'piece' is needed to gain,
'Peace' and satisfaction.

'Might' means to have strength or power.
'Might' also means maybe.
Which almost seems to suggest that,
It's stronger to be shady.

'Evil' is a term we usually,
Think of as the worst.
Yet 'evil' actually spells out 'live',
When letters are reversed.

But this one seems to make some sense,
Although it may seem awkward;
'Cause doing 'evil' simply means,
The way you 'live' is backward.

Some words within our language have,
Such subtle double meanings;
Our using them can convey,
Something more than what it's seeming.

But knowing definitions of,
These double edged words,
Can help you better comprehend them,
When they're used or heard.

# Questions of Human Worth

We all have different ways of measuring somebody's value. This poem poses questions to the reader to address his or her standard of determining that value.

# Questions of Human Worth

How do you tell what your worth is to others?
By what scale do you use?
Or what ruler to measure?
How do you determine one's value, from another?
Of which way do *you* choose,
To tell trash from a treasure?

Does material wealth tell you who is worth more?
Or the gold on the neck?
Or the rings on the hands?
Are the cars that one drives what is used to keep score?
Does it earn you respect?
Does it make you 'The Man'?

Does the circle of people you have in your life,
Give you more to live for,
Or a sense of some meaning?
Does their influence bring you to do wrong, or right?
Do they take or give more?
Of which way are they leaning?

Does the number you've had of the opposite sex,
Give you something of pride?
Keeps the ego intact?
Does the carnal conquest signify your success?
Or a place just to hide,
Something else one may lack?

And what of the learning that you may have acquired?
A degree from a college,
Or a doctorate perhaps?
Does an education make human worth higher?
Though it's good to have knowledge,
Isn't worth more than that?

Does the money you have in your bank account,
Mean your value is greater,
Than all of the rest?
With the cash you have stashed, and all its amount,
When you meet your Creator,
Won't its value be less?

While a few have a lot, and so many have little,
Seems to put us at odds,
With each person's quality.
We are all left to figure the difficult riddle:
How to understand God,
With human inequality.

When it's all said and done and your life is expired,
And we've left all possessions,
Behind us on Earth;
I hope He grants answers to those who've aspired,
In search to solve questions,
Of our value, and worth.

# The God of All Religions

I'm going to go out on a limb here and
proclaim that there is only one God, and
that God is far more powerful than all
forms of organized religion combined.

# The God of All Religions

The greatest mystery of all time.
The answers most have yet to find.
Conceptualizing God,
Has challenged all of humankind.

His power doesn't have an end.
Far greater than the minds of men,
Could ever think to grasp;
Too much for us to comprehend.

All the many types of religions,
Are mere cultural renditions,
That contradict each other,
And end up causing more division.

But there's just one God Almighty.
His children spend too much time fighting.
We need to focus more,
On all the wrongs we should be righting.

Although we call Him different names,
His oneness still remains the same.
Jehovah, Jah, Allah,
No term or word could quite contain;

The power of His majesty.
Creator of the galaxies.
Our conflicts of religion,
Causes sacrilegious travesties.

Instead of doing what is worse,
Those of all faiths need to converse;
And work to understand,
Our places in **HIS** universe.

God is always and forever.
If we want to know Him better,
His wisdom is found in learning,
To live in harmony, together.

# Remember Me?

This one is written in the voice of the Truth reminding people if its presence.

# Remember Me?

I'm the truth that you distorted.
I'm false stories you reported.
You didn't think no one records it,
But I saw you since the start.

I'm the fact that you denied,
When you chose to tell a lie.
So there should be no wondering why,
When it all comes apart.

Remember me?

I'm the problems you neglected.
I'm the bribe that you collected.
I'm the alibi you protected,
Even when you knew it's wrong.

So many times the truth you've twisted,
You probably forgot that I existed.
But I'm here to tell you, in case you've missed it,
That I've been here all along.

Remember me?

I'm the promise that you broke.
I'm the conflict you provoked.
You played it off like it's a joke,
And you hid it all from sight.

I'm that undiscovered sin,
That you buried deep within.
But even though you may pretend,
It *will* be brought to light.

Remember me?

I'm the skeletons in your closet.
I'm your fraudulent deposit.
Though no one else may know who caused it,
I witness each and all.

So all deceptions you're creating,
And lies you've been articulating,
I will be patiently awaiting,
At the bottom of your fall.

Remember me?

I'm the rug you swept things under.
I see your scheme. I've got your number.
Though everybody else may wonder,
I look straight in your mind.

Don't blame it on your circumstances.
You have been given many chances.
The devil that you chose to dance with,
Will burn you every time.

Remember me?

The truth is just not to be toyed with.
Just hear your conscience when it voices.
And check the mirror with your choices.
Be true to what reflects!

Although you can lie to your senses,
With self-delusional defenses,
You still must face the consequences,
In this life, and the next.

Remember me!

# Living Forever

This poem is to help you be
mindful of your eternal self.

# Living Forever

Have you ever really thought about Forever?
It's really hard to comprehend,
Something that will not ***ever*** end.

'Cause this life often changes like the weather.
So many things we've trusted in,
Did not last when we needed them.

But do not let those disappointments blind you.
People lack the ability,
Of such infallibility.

May the truth within these words serve to remind you,
That the core of your identity,
Will last throughout infinity.

Beneath your flesh and bone is found your Soul.
That part of you that never dies,
And can't be seen by human eyes.

It is completely under your control.
And by your actions will decide,
The place of where it will reside.

The world we live in is just temporary.
Possessions that a person has,
Were never really meant to last.

That's why it should be treated secondary.
'Cause everything we see will pass,
Like sands go through an hourglass.

Please do not think that life ends when you're gone.
Of this you should be made aware,
So that you can be well prepared.

Your essence will continue to live on.
Forevermore, you'll still be there,
To spend Eternity, somewhere.

# Prayer of Understanding

Earnest supplications for what
all of us stand in need of.

# Prayer of Understanding

Eternal God our Father, please help me to see,
The world as it is, not as I wish it to be.
Reveal to me whatever You put me here to do,
'Cause I would do it that much better, if I only knew.

Since You made me, You know all my flaws and desires.
Help me do Your true will, without growing tired.
Please empower my virtues to be stronger than the rest of me,
So that I may fulfill what You have as my destiny.

Please protect me from Satan and his fiery arrows,
As I earnestly try to walk the path straight and narrow.
Please keep my family safe, and those I pray for from harm.
Help my nerves to stay calm when there's no need for alarm.

I sincerely repent for the wrongs that I've done,
And the trespasses I've committed against anyone.
I wish more than to feel that You've truly forgiven me,
But to do what it takes for Your Spirit, to live in me.

Please bless my mind so that I make better choices.
May I hear You speak audibly above all other voices.
When the plans go off course, may I not search for fault,
But of what I can do to bring a positive result.

There are so many things I witness that really seem wrong.
Help me make sense of it all, so that I can stand strong.
When the darkness of the world makes it hard to see clearly,
May Your presence remind me to keep faith and hope near me.

In the name of Your Son, and the blood that He shed,
Help me follow His example, and the words that He said.
May I never be afraid, embarrassed, or ashamed,
To stand boldly and firmly in the power of His name.

Help me focus my efforts to achieve worthwhile goals,
And to bring inner peace to my body and soul.
Please grant me strength and wisdom so that I may understand.
To You *be* the power and glory,
Forever
Amen.

# The Midnight Phoenix

Merriam-Webster's Collegiate Dictionary defines a phoenix as 'a legendary bird that lived 500 years, burned itself to ashes, and rose alive from the ashes to live another period'. This poem uses the characteristics of this mythical creature in describing the complete fulfillment of the gospel.

# The Midnight Phoenix

Crushed by the weight of the world on His shoulders.
Pushed down to Hell as the wicked get bolder.
He carries the torch as the darkness grows colder.
The Phoenix will rise as a warrior, and soldier.

Locked in a prison designed for the mind.
Forced to look up to things that are crimes.
He's now broken free, and unshackled the binds!
The Phoenix is rising, for now is the time.

Out from the ashes is formed a new face,
To bring hope to the hopeless of our struggled race.
With both mighty power, and angelic grace;
He returns to reclaim his rightful place.

He conquered the cross and arose for salvation,
Of those who are deaf, dumb, and blind from damnation.
Two thousand years later, same problems were facin',
As the souls of the saints cry for their vindication.

After having to die again, and again,
After being the prey of centuries of sin,
After feeling like the torment would just never end,
Comes the rebirth of righteousness, destined to win.

Hoodwinked, bamboozled, and once led astray,
Our ancestors looked to the Lord and would pray,
That sometime before never, would come this very day!
Their sufferings and struggles have paved us the way.

But our enemy now, is the one in the mirror.
We all need to focus to see things more clearer.
We must recognize things aren't as they appear or,
We'll be left behind as the rapture draws nearer.

So ready yourselves! There's a war we must fight!
Use Ephesians armor to strengthen your might.
As best as you can, hold onto what's right,
For the Phoenix returns at the stroke of Midnight.

I really hope you've enjoyed reading these poems. May they truly
bear a positive influence on your life.

# Special Thanks

David Claggett
Elishua Lewis
Michael Hall
Felix Samnyeme
Sondra Barksdale
Karen Vanzego-James
Linda Brooks
Anne Jhoon-Yen
Nancy New

Evelyn Ramos Lee
Marla Mernin
Estefania Pozzi Porter
Nicholas Jones
Gregory Davis

Winston Maison
Kenneth Moore
Anthony Martin
Gregory Terrell
Dwayne Smith
Vincent K. Smith

Reverend Dr. Grainger Browning, Jr.
Reverend Dr. Jo Ann Browning
Reverend Marcus Washington
Kenneth Chambers

The Love of my Life
My Beloved Parents
The Holy Trinity

Melissa Jones
Barbara Thompson
Claudia Payne
Adelaide Webb
Michelle Schutz
Aretha Brockett
Laticia Cunningham
Ramona Miles
Gerald Guieb

James Scruggs
Patricia Campbell
Starleata Marshall
Comfort Berkeley
Christopher Baugh

William Shackleford
Smiley Shackleford
Michael Jones
West Coleman
Albert 'Sarge' Cooks

Dr. Lee Crump
Dr. Walter R. McCollum
Darryl and Teresa Gordon
Bill Ferinde

9 780979 140624